Fitzroy North 3068

Also by Yvette Henry Holt

Anonymous Premonition 2008

Yvette Henry Holt

Yvette Henry Holt heralds from the Yiman, Wakaman and Bidjara nationsof Queensland. A multi-award-winning poet, editor, essayist, and accomplished social landscape photographer, Yvette's writings have been translated into multiple languages for more than two decades both online and traditional publishing format—the recipient of the David Unaipon Award 2005, Scanlon Prize for Indigenous Poetry 2008, Kate Challis RAKA Award 2010, Victorian Premier's Literary Award for Indigenous Writing 2008, and recipient of the Queensland Writers Centre Johnno Award 2024.

With avidity and passion Yvette advocates for and facilitates workshops nationally and internationally on the poetics of Indigenous cultural space, Indigenous environmental narratives, editing and publishing.

Yvette best describes herself as the occasional poet.

Yvette Henry Holt

Fitzroy North 3068

UPSWELL

First published in Australia in 2026
by Upswell Publishing
Perth, Western Australia
upswellpublishing.com

Upswell operates in the city of Perth, on ancient country of the Whadjuk people of the Noongar nation who remain the spiritual and cultural custodians of this beautiful land. We acknowledge their continuing connection to country and express gratitude to elders past and present for their strength and creativity ... Always was, always will be, Aboriginal land.

ISBN: 978-0-6459840-7-1

A catalogue record for this book is available from the National Library of Australia

Cover design by Chil3, Fremantle
Typeset in Foundry Origin by Lasertype
Printed by McPherson's Printing Group

The following poems have been published previously:

'disembarking bees' and 'ēel-ongated' published online *Verity La La ICONCLAST*, May 2025 https://verityla.com/

'In the Middle of Analysis' commissioned by *Cordite Poetry Review*, June 2022 http://cordite.org.au/

'mother(s) native tongue' Highly Recommended Oodgeroo Noonuccal Indigenous Poetry Prize 2018, published *Overland Literary Journal* online 2018 https://overland.org.au/

'yeperenye notes' commissioned by *Red Room Poetry* online Poetry Object 2018 https://redroompoetry.org/; 'yeperenye notes' published in *Guwayu – For All Times* Magabala Books 2020

for mother, my first teacher

What cannot be said above all must not be silenced but written.

Jacques Derrida

Endorsements for *Fitzroy North 3068*

Fitzroy North 3068 opens with a provocation: *Can you keep a secret?* Because this collection heaves with them – confessional in the truest sense. Yvette Henry Holt's poems traverse a psychic and geographic cartography from Inala to Footscray, Athens to London. A "proud aboriginal indigenous native black sovereign woman of colour" whose pronouns are "me /myself /and I", Holt writes through memory, identity, and matrilineal inheritance, conversing with ghosts, ancestors, poets, muses, and the archetypal inhabitants of her unconscious mind. Erotic, spiritual, irreverent, and unflinchingly intelligent, *3068* teases the reader by concealing as much as it reveals. I dare you to take your place on the chaise lounge of Holt's analytic poetry and read this book as it "reads you" back.

Michele Seminara

An extraordinarily powerful, authentic and highly original exploration of memory, *Fitzroy North 3068* is an important collection from a major literary voice.

Robbie Coburn

A warning: this poetry collection is rebellious... erotic, elegant, erudite, expansive. Endlessly inventive, brimming with allusions and wit. *Fitzroy North 3068* is a book uncomfortable in the best possible way. Occasionally, prophetic. Enter it at your own peril, because it goes as deep and wide and wild as a fine psychoanalysis does. Having read it, I feel spiritually richer. It is a gift to readers.

Lee Kofman

Fitzroy North 3068 is a profound collection of poems that at first taps you on the shoulder to remind you to be present but as you read on the tap gets heavier until you can no longer take it and face what you've been ignoring for years. Yvette Henry Holt's poems are a gift to us all, especially for those who are seeking the truth.

Magan Magan

Yvette Holt's metaphors are spellbinding: a book of *stone in peach* truths and *September honeycomb*, all *footstep memory - no compass required*, where the pages read you. Join the poet *ankled by mangroves in herstory*, then converse with galaxies as lighthouse keepers receive tangelo gifts. Melding language and spirit, Yvette Henry Holt has risen to the celestial soul-dance that is *Fitzroy North 3068*.

Anna Jacobson

Fitzroy North 3068 is a work of fiery and dazzling beauty. In both style and form it expands what might conventionally be considered 'poetry', exploring memoir, psychoanalysis and psychogeography to celebrate the everyday sacred. Holt twists, wrestles and even bullies language into new shapes: playful, haunting and erotic, bursting one way, then another, always wrong-footing while at the same time delighting the reader. Literature, Indigeneity, Judaism; time, memory and faith; childhood, motherhood, family; the urban and the desert; the light and the mist. Yvette Henry Holt is inevitably a political writer, yet her politics are celebratory rather than fashionably grim: this is a splendid journey, wandering and acrobatic, into the molten core of language, wisdom and experience.

Luke Stegemann

Contents

Introduction

The following pages contain names of people who are no longer living, it is with profound respect and sensitivity that I carry their living memory through select chapters. With cultural reverence and collective *spirit* I acknowledge the Yiman, Wakaman and Bidjara peoples of my parents' ancestral lands and inland river waters, a continuum of flowing memories unbound by time never to recede.

Much of the contents of *Fitzroy North 3068* have been handwritten and locked inside volumes of personal journals and sporadic diaries over the span of more than fifteen years, these pages have been consciously dissected and psychoanalytically re-threaded across all states and territories of Australia as well as continents near and far. For the most part the following chapters have been intentionally well hidden from natural light, therefore assemblance of these words has long been cradled and held within the confinements of my own internal custody, uncomfortable truths thawed by mirroring shadows.

I acknowledge Wurundjeri Woi Wurrung Elders and Aboriginal members of the wider Fitzroy community's pre-settlement to present day; along my perforated journey of reflection, these lands have been a returning to place, a returning to a long-awaited subconscious shelter of past, present and future.

It is on the streets of Fitzroy, Fitzroy North, Brunswick and surrounding suburbs that much of my being seeped through these hessian chapters of psychoanalysis and psychogeographical reflections, and still, like you, I rise.

Poetic license has been discreetly embroidered to protect *spirit*,
weaver of silence.

When you know, *you know*!

Yvette Henry Holt

Can you keep a secret?

Well, can you?

Chapter I

Poetics of Anatomical Space

The great function of poetry is to give back to
us the situations of our dreams

Gaston Bachelard

Poetic Dissidence

Go gentle when you
first enter her.
Do not thunderstorm
your way into the
lyrical membrane of a
muscular nub that
whisks solely for the
mooring of a dislocated
tongue cloaked only in
subconscious
asphalt.

Be brave but not so brave
that you uptilt these
bodice dreams in lieu
of knowing swells and
the ineffable hunger for
someone else's
all things cellar and attic.

Take your moment, there
is no such thing as rush
for Pachelbel will
continue to roam up and
down your confessional
spine in Canon D Major
whether you are present
inside these underground
dream crates or not.

Centimetre yourself through
these pages like unhurried
treacle upon damper.
Inquire like mulberry
silkworms
at the brow of
monsoonal hush
unsuspecting,
unafraid,
deliberate.

And remember this
above all else,
promise the poet
that you
can keep a secret,
as safe as —
stone in peach.

For I tell you truthfully
friend,
the silent woman is
only ever an eggshell
away
from cocking the poetic
chamber.

Directions for Use:

Author's notes:
Position book where best suited
for optimal discomfort.

At any time, feel
free to unweld the author's mind
with a traditional rust-free
can-opener.

Hold collection upside down for no
more than twenty-seconds at a time,
if words do not drop like clout nails
from accordion margin then straw
contents backwards commencing
from chapter three.

Between interval, please allow for
one to two hundred years of
self-infusion to seep into your
pores (resistance) is not optional.

Reduce, simmer and then return
author to the boil. Repeat
as necessary.

Additionally, once lukewarm
to taste, reader may wish to add
sage honey for anti-inflammatory
colonial, psychiatric sweetness.
Be sure to stir well (clockwise) of course.

When not in use, store in a cool,
dry place – preferably out of
direct sunlight.

Deposit poet into anything other than
a national museum or airtight
container.

Publisher's note:
Once opened, you cannot unopen.

Epilogue

The indelible Finke River
an estuary of arid vertical roots

{–}

a place in the sun where theology curves
and the ocean
…forgotten

{–}

an elegy of wonting postcards
franked by garnet sands
were scriptures bronze
like kerosene lampstands
hulking upon the wick of an iron sermon

{–}

come Sundays
not so high on the hill
behind the pre-war morgue
you and I, we whisper skin on skin
our backs annexed
against minacious winds
of Wittenberg rains
droplets of genetic hymns
cursing downward
into salts of no return

{–}

Journal entry: 20th December, 2015

Church bells hammer, meanwhile, Babylonian gills propel towards the fluid artery of Simpson Desert. Mid-morning pews dissolve into full bloom; here I crouch, taking a squat on the sunbeaming latrine, dustpan light slits through a hanging doorframe; noting an army of spangled caterpillars migrating their way into the elbows of unmarked trunks.

My once deliberate sanity, all but now consumed.

The air, hollow.

The river rising!

Belly button thirsty.

{–}

you and I

kneeling by shade

preaching in German

releasing in verse

way back when

a baptism of unquenchable fire

desire

{–}

Journal entry extract: 22nd December, 2024

Reflecting on a life that once was, understanding that not all fires require rain.

Auf Wiedersehen, mein Flussfreund

disembarking bees

on the first day of spring
in the earliest possible hour
rain will mizzle;

----

tapping at your window
an empty flask
full of chutzpah
roaming russet eyes
and a wandering chin;

----

boney candles will whistle you
from down the hallway
you will rise,
like September honeycomb
oh, how you shall rise;

for.
you.
/i will sting;

~~Heresy~~ Her\sea

Just as sea urchins are aligned
with the biological calling of a
mustardy full moon rising
so too are poetesses,

beneath nocturnal shoreline
floorboards
we gather like alphabetical clams
heightened by knee bones
ankled by mangroves
waiting in canopy for
monarchal
tide to arrive

squid ink glazing
between teeth

spilling dance and prose
until we can spill no more,
stretching and kneading
sandcastles across garret
sheets of wide-brown clay feet
atop arthropodal hamlets
a coattail page,

beneath the sea's
quietening parlance
a herstorical rage

silhouetting with moon
untailored by breath
rib caged by waters
poetica lunae
feasting her\seas
waiting as patiently as
ancient tongues,
the giver of – giving

note to self

Haley's Comet 1986

I am no closer to understanding
you.
An intimate valley.
A sealed keyhole.
I cannot get close to you.
I live with the not knowing.
I never wanted all of you, just
some of you.
Not the whole passing phenomena,
just the tail end.

Only enough to tell the galaxy before
bedtime that
I tasted you – parts of you
and it was delicious.

`ēel-ongated

Winter's dilettante stampedes lake:;

eels' jasmine into poets:;

unwinding laneways
overlap lipped algae
in full costume:;

bottlebrush and
sweet mock orange
ignite all apostrophes,
leafing tally-ho 'ash:;

café curtains masque
with symbolic allegory:;

side-gates resurrect into
thirty pieces of frozen silver:;

footprints wodge into
tiles of shoebox ice:;

beating beneath a rindless brunet surface
unmetered syllables erupt with inferno:;

`ēel
lengthened, ravenous, librettists
two jaws, one true heart, no scales:;

A Conjuring¿

Statutory Declaration:
I, Yvette Henry Holt, do solemnly declare
that I currently reside with more dead poets
than that of any other poetic impostor
I know of living or otherwise.
Furthermore, I solemnly declare that each
one of them from time to rhyme take
jack-in-the-box turns in gathering around
my hand-me down well-weathered
Queen Anne three-and-a-half legged
Tasmanian oak poster bed.

My guests, arriving as they do,
processionally on the mint of 1:00am,
jangling chapters and raising Cain from
a field of epic genre-bending seminal
poets,
pleading with me to scribe alongside
them in total pitch licorice,
behind cemetery tiles,
beyond the cottontail back door.

I do as they ask.

When first editions come calling,

one must always do as they ask.

I am neither taken nor arriving, the conjuring

of the de-see-ease`d are only here and there for

a flickering of woven cloth,

herein lay our thumbprints…

borrow; but do not follow.

Signed: ***Y H Holt***

Witnessed: *Sylvia, Octavio, Emily, Pablo, Rainer, Kath, Anne, Adrienne, Mary, Audre, June, Jean, Charles, Ted, Dorothy*

– et cetera and so on

Dated: *From here to uncertainty*

Suburban Lighthouse

#1
Once upon a mime, on the very odd occasion our
neighbourly lighthouse keeper would serve me
homecooked suppers, platters of mountainous
saffron seasoned rice and fatty meaty stews all
delivered on returnable disposable dinner plates.

#2
The family backyard grows citrusy wild all year round,
a living breathing suburban corner of vitamin c and all
that tang tipping the mason jars.

#3
Meanwhile, I give the lighthouse keeper a little something, something
from time to time

a lime

a lemon

a tangelo

a tangerine

a mandarin

a ruby red orange

a fistful of cumquats.

#4
Journal entry:
4:44am, 6th October 2021
The kettle boils with regal infuriation. I am wandering around the dining room, unpeeling hiccup dreams of Heathcliff chasing my once crinkle-free corselette underlays across defrosting westerly willowy windy moors.

Awake, poetically-wide-awake!
I am shadowless, legless, and barely touching the ceiling, the steaming water blows like a ship in the wardrobe that has all but lost its northern star.

The kitchen rises like a public bathhouse – downstairs a laundry room door is knocking from the inside out just begging for attention, palm tree dungarees grow awash with urban myths and staining legends.

Not a teaspoon to be found!

From the mid-louvre corner I note a certain curtain twitch,
the lighthouse keeper is also awake, no doubt wandering the gangplank of his early morning call.

He too must be having dreams of Catherine rolling down the pristine greenery of a northern English countryside in search of her beloved Heathcliff.

The stage is set.
Tea for two.
Marmalade for one.
The curtains must open!

Perhaps this is all just lighthouse etiquette in neighbourly sign language, perhaps it is simply a suburban buffer to first light post rapid eye movement?

Perhaps not?

#5
Confessions of a wandering middle-aged daughter.
I am all but out of touch with urban domestic bliss;
house-sitting, housekeeping, house-wanking,
house-painting, house-mating, house-calling is all but
unfamiliar territory to me.

I remind myself that I have lived in dongas, dressing-table drawers and desert tree shanties with wild brumbies that mated like clockwork after 10pm directly outside the porthole of my abode for over twelve years and years and years, and for most of those remote desert nights I slept
just as the dolphins do,
all smiles with one eye open.

#6
Deciding to respond to the unnerving curtain, and so, from above the re-marbled kitchen benchtop I offer up a nipple, not just any old nipple, the perky one, the demure show pony thimble, the ménage à trois favourite – a fruitful symbol of ageless erotica fuelled by wuthering goodwill.

The lighthouse keeper's lace-drop curtains ever so subtly widen, medieval hallways roar with borrowed pelicans from someone else's dreams, and just then a litany of cutlery pelts from the river of teaspoons plonking themselves haphazardly across the materiality of house, home, obedience, belonging and space.

#7
And then just like that,
a kitchen ocean dissolves.

Planetarium dreams refold into
the pantry of domestic white
vinegar and salt reduced vegemite.

Reassembling oneself back to reality;
there are dishes to be done.
Benchtops to be wiped.
Floors to be swept.
A backdoor landing, thirsting for a mop.

The mini coupé nipple
retreats
to bathrobe at-ease.

The neighbourly lighthouse keeper
fades into freckles of anatomical
pre-dawn
besprinkle.

Brontë for a fleeting moment alive and
swell in the working-class
south-western 'burbs of Brisbane.

The coffee grows cold – as do I.

No ashes to see here,
just recycled dust.

All but a rather scenic
dream within a dream.

eavesdropping

earthworms
turning mind inside
out

digging for minerals

pumice frontal
lobe

language
drips

dwelling
impulse
cocooning
moist leaf litter

populous
nitrogen
liquid
fortifies

molten poetry

porously
necessary
musical
diaphragm

tunnels on repeat

rhythmic
invertebrate

floating in water
nearby

warm occipital
lava

green ants
combat heavy grey metal

punching above
their sporing weight

.The Knowing

Perhaps like you

I only know

what I do not know

&

what I do not know

is done

&

what I know for certain can no longer be undone

Sea of Tranquillity (Mare Tranquillitatis)

The first time I ever opened
my mouth for a /'wʊmən/
an adult female human being
I felt parts of my body
tectonically exit this
universe and resettle onto
a fine celestial body surface
{{{{{{{{{{{{{{{{{{{{{{{{{{{{{{{{{{{
that was one small step
for this woman
}}}}}}}}}}}}}}}}}}}}}}}}}}}}}}}}}}}
one giant leap
for my kind

THE ~~END~~ BEGINNING

Chapter II

The Müse

A little bit of light pushes away a lot of darkness

Jewish proverb

Two in a room

Sunday morning reading room /
autumn sills /
north nor' easterly /

Octavio /
Neruda /
dashing sun /

the muse sipping karkedeh
slowly in Spanish /

grandmother, silent in Hebrew /

& then there is I
the occasional poet
unbottled by chapter and chalk /

Myüzings

The sea is always the sea

      never the belfry

no amount of handwringing
from sight will ever

be clever enough to escape
its poetic carpentry

speak of mountains
chiselling skies
with uncomplicating hands

remove all thread from
thrumming lungs across
shivering
forests as they
too
have waited long,
long enough to have their
way with language

walk out the seasons
with poetic consent

                  by day

footing ungated words
upon throw rugs of nature's
volcanic paperclips by night

heal
with each step
by the whetstones of Andes feet

but the sea

soul of the sun

stars

yareakh

oh – muse,

depths of you

will always be sea

The Tower of Blue Horses

What appears spectral today will be natural tomorrow – Franz Marc

blue horses surround – said the alchemist to the muse

friends laughter

strangers loyal

adventurists

steadfast intense numinous

spirit weaver

soul

companion

protector

chef

confidanté

masseuse

strength

fragility life freedom

motherless loss love

Mother Complex

1945–2019 | 1951–2025

the muse & i
shall carry incomplete
poems
of our mothers for now &
always.

wearing their memory
an ouroboros wreath.
mummy
back-strapped
to reeds of
undercut preconsciousness.

birth-marking
continents of
burial & joie de vivre,
mum
there will be truth.

as only daughters of the
devoured can speak
of.

the silent finch,
home

‘,

holding mother’s hand

all at

once

a returning

to nest

Ross River

Dear Muse,

Between first-light and sunrise
therein carves an unmasked trail
which I tend to sleepwalk
hand-in-hand
with my Wakaman grandmother /

filing by timeworn knuckles
of sandpaper figs and melaleucas
clouds,
complete with emerald chatter
nearing a full-bodied waterway
brimming with poesy and paean /

just before sparrow messages the
tawny frogmouth
meet me by the river's bend /

for you and you only I will
breathe knowing verse into
upstream gills of moses perch /
mangrove snapper, dusky
flatheads, big-eyed trevally and
sui generis
black jewfish.

Prophecy of the Pig

Here in Choquequirao, where eagles circle sun
            tethered pig feathers bone upon bone

Chapter III

Treatment in Haiku

I think haiku is the most beautiful form of poetry I know

John Lennon

isolation rooms
a place where haiku grows wild
inside winter's chest

exhuming childhood
into darklyness we play
tan moon will soon rise

scrubbing bathtub poems
sunlight liquid drips in vein
syringing quatrains

poetics of space
slipper her from room to room
swallowing me whole

roamin' catholic
hovering low above me
music bittersweet

psychotherapy
where wolf and lamb coagulate
pulling woollen teeth

flying into naarm
disembowelling egoism
transference en route

half-slip lane café
yanking my order thrice over
double-shot, on white

brunswick street fitzroy
to her door these scars erupt
on the couch i sin

tall tea ships set sail
irreversibly wading
towards my navel

early morning tram
jars full of antibodies
the next stop is mine

you and i decide
to uncouple privately
in silence we stall

for sale one used womb
hysterically gendered
inquire deep within

that mirror woman
i know her by reflection
she lures you to me

psychotherapists
are sometimes poets on paid leave
one canoe, two oars

they say home is where
the rain is, fitzroy north tastes
better than london

Chapter IV

Psychogeography – a walk through words

I haven't been everywhere, but it's on my list

Susan Sontag

Introduction

1970
conceived on Jaggera/Yuggera Country
Home sweet home

1971
birthed on Turrbal Country
Royal Brisbane Women's Hospital

reattached by Maiwar

body of the eternal

unwinding Brown Serpent

River, Brisbane

4077 The Dérive

My love for walking here there and everywhere first commenced with motherly-daughterly trepidation, the letting go into the unknown from the front gate of our family home in 1975 when at the curious age of four, I placed one tiny foot in front of the other inside my leather patent toddler t-strap casual princess sienna beige shoes to journey into what I believed to be the other side of beckoning stars.

This is the mother-love, which is one of the most moving and unforgettable memories of our lives.

There was mother standing behind me saying 'Go on Missy you can do it', and there was Kevvy (eight-years old) waiting at the gates of Sunday School for his kid sister, his string-bean copper tone arms outstretched as far as they could, his hands clapping together like a theatrical seal, anticipating my running into his heart.

Sunday School was less than one hundred metres from our home. That astonishing morning kicked off my love for all things on foot by curiosity – I was taken in by surroundings of different coloured letterboxes, muddy driveways, grassy driveways, tapestry painted plant pots, unopened venetian blinds and begonias living in harmony next to unrivaled hibiscuses.

My blossoming inhalation of walking memory was beyond instrumental, it was just as Lao Tzu had prescribed –
"A journey of a thousand miles begins with a single step."

Who could have imagined that one sunny Sunday morning a delighted four-year old girl would literally fall head of rubber sole heel with the impressionable joy – psychology of geography (psychogeography) and all that the unplanned world had to offer was hers for the taking.

The rest as they ought to say is *herstory.*

Philopappos Hill

(Hill of the Muses) Athens

in pulsing silence

by canyon sinew

three forest peaks

taking their turn

cradling lap

psalming hair

grapeseed moonlight

each imperfect opening

mouthless before liprise

lesbos isle by lyrical osmosis

kneeling departure

Sappho has spoken

yeperenye notes

last night, by the falling waistcoat
of a half-caste desert moon
discreetly, deliberately
i heel away from somnolent flutes
water-coloured caterpillars and testaments of olde
\
into a floral jar of untitled clay-pans and annotated spinifex
inhaling burgundy-stained pages of handwritten riverbeds
silently, incessantly
quilling louvred hours of jaundiced memories
\
by the rising ceremonial seas of ante meridiem
echoing curlews ribbon my desiccated tongue
mirroring speech
if only occasionally
quite lucidly, most insanely
i delight in the sweet palm of darkness

Pantai Merah

I should have told you

sooner rather than later

that unlike you – my love

I was never a strong swimmer

an uncompromisingly seasoned walker – yes

but just add me to nonnative ocean waters and I dematerialise out of sunsight /

some four hours away from the sleepy

fishing village of Labuan Bajo

some three hundred metres offshore

from you

I had no business sinking in waters

that were all but a stranger to me /

our chartered diesel boat hosts

noted that my sea-less

sea legs

were wearily untreading

waters of feigned docility

amidst Venus's descending barb /

slowly but surely

picture-perfect unfiltered reefs

depicting desktop
coral specks
captured the decline
of my pixelating lower body /

feet cursing
knees praying /

no flagstone path of
submerging medieval
granite
to impale my indigenous
shins against /

no raised dorsal fin to
accuse of prodding
these descending aboriginal hips /

no marine constabulary
could return me swiftly enough
to your sun-burning
when Irish thighs are smiling
shanks
as you waved me handstand down
across a shoreline of intoxicative
rosé sands /

turquoise pride was going
under – fast
faster than a
ten-foot long
neighbouring Komodo dragon
in dire need of a
good vegan feed

gasping beneath unedited
first nations
air quotes
bubbling just above
someone else's tribal surface /

all is well that
somehow
floats well
a return to certainty – my love
Of that I am shore /

Mile End E1 4NS

Novo Beth Chaim

For Dr Ananya Mishra

beneath soundless rain,
measuring each footstep
tip-toeing in between
English moss
&
Sephardic mason
crosswording a field
of oneiric worlds
I journal an acre
of merchant weft
lamenting surnames
persecution
immigration
theology
industry
upon
economics
upon
settlement
upon
new world traders

upon
Cromwell and Country

this eighteenth-century heart of mine
heels among London's tombstone east
where inscribed hand-cut letterheads
preside over quarried slate gravestones

and there she sits,
low-noon
out-of-body,
full of rise
∨
the occasional poet
thinking out loud
writing in silence
∧
postured by winter's eyes
looking over shoulder
waiting on a friend

Memphis, Tennessee

Home of the Blues
Birthplace of Rock 'n' Roll
I could not have been happier than sharing Memphis
with you, pickpocketing every plate of sight & sound
vis-à-vis Memphian rhythm

counting Peabody Ducks twice daily,
rolling in elm, sweetgum and poplar while
picnicking by the oesophagus of the one and holy
mighty Mississippi River
her southern narrative lining the corners of my
fitted sheets

look at me, gavotting like a woman possessed
across garden beds that never sleep,
detouring away from streetcars overflowing
with southern charm
calling your name to
climb on board

jealousy is a curse you say,
a curse, that I have yet to defeat
I reply

wise men says that moody blues
roll all over suspicious minds
as we slowly cruise
down the boulevard of
Shelby County

retracing each footstep inside the
body library of a
Jungle Room,
a different kind of cell

looking for clues, meandering through
everything in
everything out
not a nickel of Mr E. Presley
to be found

you and I capturing the night
walking towards the creed of
Beale Street
heart of the bluest
scriptures

these fire escape legs
obeying every chord being plucked,
every cowbell being rung

everybody who was anybody lined up
for blocks
to enter
143 Beale Street

you,
– like an alabastrine panther moving
through the crowd
peacocked chest
and belt-buckled the size of
Texas,
swingingly confident

you,
– knowing the club like the back
of your paw

you,
– with your stout ego wrapped shapely
around my naïve youthful stretchmark free
early twenty-something waist

and then there is only you and I,
us,
at the table of a living King

you,
– with your beautiful alarm clock mouth
introduced me to the reigning
Monarch of Blues
Mr B.B. King in the flesh and
He in turn introduced me to a
Lucille

forget the barbecued vegan ribs
forget catfish on the kosher table
forget that I am tongue-tied and twisted
internally like a lone tornado too distant
to quantify the impact of His Majesty

thereafter I walked out the days in
Memphis
home of the bluest blues
poeticising the nights

hiding like a saint forgetting
to sin
across the road from
Sun Records Studio
splashed only in Earl Grey tea
shelled inside the biceps of your
Louisianan confederacy

I, completely cuckoo for you
on paperback rooftops of
ash-traying
blasphemous
neon shadows
in search of an
olive green martini moon

all the while
our preface hearts
lay in state
making sanitorium promises
to each other
by the beak of an unfurnished sunrise

every ——————————thing

was just as it should be
inside chasing daisies
upside-upside worlds

the green light of the story,
walk your path
own it and remember,
rear vision never lies

Heptonstall, West Yorkshire

No map, no wind, not a
single bird seeking freedom
brought me to you on that
arctic day in late January

I found you by scent,
inside circle dreams
mashed from spinifex
and polyester spat ink

Sylvia, I bring paper and pencil
to your final writing place,
resting by the lefthand corner pocket
of St Thomas a' Beckett's church
a tame intimate English breakfast village
shadowed in perennial forget-me-nots of
your larger than life – death

sitting silly at the bedhead of your
watery grave
as quiet as a
churchyard mouse
I want to do some digging
a gardener of your whispers
by hand
by ear
by neck
by knees
by the reflection of my own
poetic complexion

Sylvia, the grassless naked path
surrounding your lotus reclining ark
leaks with letters, fingernails,
scruffy stuffed uncuddly toys
and distant motorways of half-truths
from a world mirroring inside the
canon of your confessional words
your now forever home, a place where
wild salmon roses bleach blossoming
orange tulips
reminding the moorlands wintery
windswept months on how to survive
your deciduous pages

blood
bleeding
bled

Sylvia, in late spring I promise,
flowers will return to your sacred
sunken trove
blooming with Ariel glow

blank pages now prosper inside my
gelid lined Cambridge pockets
rustling in search of an older, newer
you
          am I really here?
          Sylvia,
          are you really there?

some say dying is an art – but I say, so is writing

Sylvia Plath 1932 – 1963
daughter of Aurelia and Otto

'Even amidst fierce flames, the golden lotus can be planted'

4078

plump seedless clouds
warble
in & out of
                                        forest
consciousness

yonic feathers
tarpaulin
                                        lake
autumn brume
menstrual leaves
                                        taproots
lapwing
& thrush

performing as
                                        silent
as truth

no geese to speak of
no cormorant to marvel at
no ripe memory to
                                        curse

What is now known as Forest Lake was once the ultimate playground of unobstructed imagination and heightened childhood adventure for entire generations of children descending from all corners of Inala / Richlands and its district outskirts.

Lorikeet Street Serviceton South once backed onto a world of wide-eyed wonder, fascination and neighbourhood camaraderie. Our tightknit possé of Inala East gathered en masse in preteen droves to hustle our thoughts across kilometres of unscripted walks deep into the virgin bushland of where Forest Lake is situated today.

Throughout the seasons of our school holidays, we walked for the most part barefoot into the tummy of the nearby woodlands, rainforest and cedar rich bush to create makeshift playhouses made from sleeping branches aligning front gardens ornamented with shrapnel that were half-buried into the unforgiving earth courtesy of the WWII US Army ordnance depot. We would go about our business and build bush humpies one day and the following day we would return with anything we could hide under our armpits to make it more comfy i.e. tablecloths, pin cushions, jars filled with torn handwritten first crush notes, and tea-towels galore.

The magical land of never-ending bush tracks we sought so fervently beneath a coughed-up galaxy of Jack in the Beanstalk trees were as real to us as the Greenbank Military Range firing off gunnery exercises in the not-so-earshot-distance to where we roamed almost daily without a care in the world, boundlessly.

Today, most days

I walk the lake,

I talk to the lake

I listen deeply to the lake

the lake and I are companions,

a companion should

always be companionable

in creativity

longevity

and solitude

trees, birds, skies, turtles, eels

in all beauty and disguise

whisper back,

Holty, you are welcome.

No need to ask;
Where have all the flowers gone?
I know by heart where the flowers
have grown,
those saplings,
they too grew me up.

I till from the core of
ungovernable
footstep memory.

t
h
e

l
a
n
d

surrenders not.

one, two — buckle my shoe

Since 1994

Brisbane to Brixton

Melbourne to Memphis

Darwin to Dubai

Cairns to Cambridge

Sydney to Seattle

Tennant Creek to Tokyo

Brunswick to Banff

Wollongong to Wellington

Auckland

Edinburgh

Tacoma

Victoria Island

Los Angeles

Whistler

Vancouver

Athens

Dhaka

New Delhi

Doha

Mumbai

Denpasar

Sacramento

Singapore

London

Kuala Lumpur

West Hollywood

three, four, knock at the door
five, six pick up sticks
seven, eight lay them straight

Fitzroy North

St Georges road

\

footpath

unhinged

birdbath

/

Brisvegas

Central Australia

Barkly Street closed

\

down the curve

sparkling wokeography

via

Gertrude Street garments

postage paid

return to suspender

/

therapy indubitably

surveys the mire of

orbital details

\

magnetic fields of

underground wine bars

harbouring loose eyes

growing vineyard lush

beneath an

unmanned

manhole

/

fiddler escapes the roof

\

this spherical mind of

Fitzroy North

cables me beyond 2.5

square kilometres

/

a borderless vessel

\

a forever compendium

awaiting poetic forceps

/

ascending with decency

nearby the undergrowth

rotunda of

Edinburgh Gardens

\

joltingly the old world

smells all brand new

inside this

longanimous chapter

/

just ask the Birrarung

\

misty

river

memory

flowing

/

always was

\

no compass required

/

In praise of reflective walking

On a windy crisp early June morning
I walked from
Southampton Street Footscray,
to Collins Street Melbourne

William Cooper – a proud
Yorta Yorta man, leader, activist, elder

William Cooper – we will never
forget your tireless indomitable pursuit
of campaigning and lobbying government
for equal rights and improved better living
conditions for Aboriginal people

William Cooper – we will never
forget your courage; and how your
memorable timeline influentially
threads across the generations
to this day

William Cooper – we will never
forget that you were a man of the
people,
your people, our people
yesterday
today
tomorrow

William Cooper – we will never
forget your unwavering tenacious
fight for human justice and civil rights

William Cooper – we will never
forget that you were a man of the
Letter(s)

William Cooper – we will never
forget how you and fellow Aboriginal
leaders organised a movement, in protest
of the 150th anniversary landing of the
First Fleet – 26th January, 1938
forever marked as the first
Aboriginal Day of Mourning,
Australian Hall, Elizabeth Street, Sydney

William Cooper – we will never
forget how you famously petitioned
the King of England (King George V),
with some 1,814 Aboriginal signatures
from across the lands, calling to action
Aboriginal representation
in the federal parliament of Australia

William Cooper – we will never
forget how the Australian Aborigines League
organised a delegation led by you to walk
from your home in Footscray to
419 Collins Street Melbourne
on the 6th December 1938, and to present a
petition protesting the mass persecution of
European Jews by Nazi Germany to the
German Consul-General,
Dr. D.W. Drechsler

World history reflects that you were *the man
who stood up to Hitler*
recognising this critically historical
movement as one of the first petitioned
protests in the world against the

pogromist actions of Nazi Germany
following the *Night of Broken Glass*
Kristallnacht

William Cooper – a son, a brother,
a husband, a father, an uncle, a cousin,
a grandfather, a great-grandfather,
a true friend to many, a man who stood
up for the rights of others when he
himself was dispossessed of inherent
citizenship rights

William Cooper – today, we
remember, honour and echo your name,
your cultural, social and political
legacy beats ardently in the chest
of humanity

William Cooper – I will never
forget the howling winds of that
winter's morn as I walked back the
hands of time seeking to find just a
morsal of solace inside a world that is
still aching,
still aching,
still,
still…still…still…aching…
aching be still…

Thank you, Mr. William Cooper.
Thank You!
Toda rabah lecha!

Chapter V

Hands of My Mother

Every Mother contains her daughter in herself and every daughter her mother and every mother extends backwards into her mother and forwards into her daughter.

Carl Jung

Mother archetype

if you came here
looking for my
mother inside me
you will not find
her.

mother flew away
22nd July, 2019
to be with her
old people
sisters
friends
and her
beloved
Kevvy.

if you are looking for healing,
stay a while…

Washing days (Larapinta)

Towels, tea-towels, odd socks
glue-stained paint-splotched
school uniforms, loose coins,
pockets of desert pebbles,
one lone marble,
a meticulously folded email address,
forgotten gum wrappers
all reign supreme over
washing days, here in Larapinta

too many towels
and not enough face washers
voluntarily mount by the
backside laundry door

Let the countdown begin;

One:
An overstuffed front loader
washing machine
bucking like a mechanical bull
at the laundry gate of liquid
and fabric softener

Two:
A chorus line of brawn cotton
looped Manchester
hanging haplessly across an
unaffixed forever in a day
uphill and down dale
outback quasi clothesline

mother hands me a cupful of pegs
mother is buried six-and-a-half-feet
under the earth adjacent to Kevin
in Brisbane.

Three:
With daughterly devotion
I accept mum's gift

Four:
I ask mother to stay a while,
instead, she dissolves into
forty-four degrees
stifling
celsius
mid
summer
desert
heat
her immediate evaporation
beading my already soak-drenched
river inlet shoulders into an inland
sea urn

Five:
I can hear the school bell
ring out for little-lunch recess
at Larapinta Primary School
where my grandchildren are by
now unwrapping their favourite
cucumber, tomato and cheese
sandwiches with love, G'andma

Six:
A menagerie of heavily soaked
desert zoo beach towels now
performatively hang to

syllable perfection
in pegging haiku 5-7-5

Seven:
Laundry day next Tuesday
will feature bedlinen,
coverlets,
four tablecloths
and one disgruntled bathing suit

Eight:
Memo to self ~
Next week, peg the laundry up
in tanka,
5-7-5-7-7

signed by *hands of my mother*
the original unsung laundress poet;

Inala East
Brisbane
Clermont
Woorabinda
Rockhampton

Nine:
Truly, my cup runneth over.

Matrilineal memory

I was born from a constellation
of aboriginal mothers,
in darkness and light
north to the south-east of
maternal meridian.

Upon birthing me
mother
held her breath
as did I.

That's all I have known.

All I will ever know is that
my mother
poured her mother onto me
"clever way" ———————————
bones.
hair.
eyes.
nails.
poetry.

shoulders.

legs.

Walk this way, if you dare…

————————————— "mother is calling"

mother(s) native tongue

We are thieves of sunlight
mother and I,
soaking in the seasonal crusts
of a south-east Queensland winter.

Layering shawls upon time
across the brim of our
cinnamon dusted Yiman Wakaman shoulders.

Hand in my hand
dutifully mother shuffles around
this garden playground,
her distant nursing home.

Deeply rooted terracotta pots
forge among crayon-coloured flowers
giving rise to an inquiring ladybug
mountaineering forbidden brown skin
exploring just below the unthreading hem line
of mother's inherent sculptured legs.

My ears hunt for a serpent butterfly echoing in distress.

My eyes miscarry.

Edging towards her beloved garden bed
the one nearest the aviary
before a manicured mattress of flora and fauna
we kneel in faith
mother and I,
but not in prayer.

Marigolds, snap-dragons, begonias, daffodils
and blooming pansies lotion my lean desert fingers
gently sailing up and down the oars of their urban throats
I tickle in delight
mother looks on
half interested
half not.

Mother begins to scribble with her tongue in a language
I do not understand.

Listening with borrowed providence to the spillage of her words
excitement bewilderment
anger
happiness
frustration
confusion
laughter
judgement
confabulation.

I am jealous.

What a recipe of speech?

You never offered me your language.

Never.

Not once.

Only occasionally you loaned me your Aboriginal-English lingo
a thorough concoction of bastardy words if ever there were,
along with conversations of the deceased premonitions of
the future
history of the Letters
mother you impress me

always in privacy,
always without witness.

Now your mind reclines into an abyss of natal sustenance
piece by piece,
your glossary so fertile.

I want to speak my mother's tongue!

That same crossword dialect for which you were forbidden to voice
post 1945 (Woorabinda Settlement).

Softly whispering to my first teacher,

I know poetry
I know stars
I have also grown to
know the sting of bees.

Mother smiles
muling away the curtains from
her silken Aboriginal Afghan-Indian eyes.

Leaning her ear towards mine
mother sighs with grand certainty
...I gave you all my stories!

Sunlight now shifts from one shoulder
to the other
casting shadows over these handwritten notes.

For the lifers of this home
morning tea is now served
in the adjacent dining room,
the one without a garden view.

I pocket a chrysanthemum
breaking its defenceless stem
between my fingers
burying seeds
inside my jacket.

Still no serpent butterfly in sight.

Mother's memory,
a silent womb
a sacred tomb
a place that will forever unbolt me.

Mother continues to hold my hand.

eidetic memory

Before I could speak,
I was little water-dreaming
listening quietly like a belly-full mosquito by mother's – paternal river
Taroom, Lower Dawson via Woorabinda

``````````````````

Five years later, I was running like goanna through dry savannah scrub
limestone bluffs and caves descending into the incalculable hands of time
by Chillagoe way, mother's maternal cradle

````````````````````

In *spirit*, daughter shall someday return to her mother's songlines

````````````````

In life, the journey begins
````````````````

Progenitor

Kempe Street, The Gap
Alice Springs 2017

tonight, i went looking for my mother
but please, don't tell anyone

i searched high and kneeled low
under the stairwell
in the bathroom
across the street

i awaited her entrance all night

the courtyard was barren
the kitchen vacant
the living room space empty of light

upstairs
inhaling skin

bedside
rosary beads unperturbed

hair rattles
bones dare not sleep

mother is here

yet i am separate

Belonging

for Cheyenne Holt

Mother, you should know
that my daughter continues
to soothe
in and out of your kitchen,

just as she did

when she was crying in your
arms as a
newborn bub
baby
toddler
infant
child
teen
mother
adult

and now
her children entwine
in and out of your
handsewn kitchen,
walking back the
generations through
cupboards of flour,
sippy cups, dining
ornaments and
scratched-up
baking trays of your
1960s
70s
80s

90s
culinary heydays

same Tupperware
same homemade apron
same handwritten recipes
different curtains

mother,
truly, you are love-d
you are strength
you are healing

hand in my daughter's hand
your kitchen, for always

our belonging

I

daughter of

Albert Holt ♡ **M**arlene (née Henry) Holt

Bidjara Yiman/Iman, Wakaman

y
v
e
t
t
e

h
e
n
r
y

h
o
l
t

thinks like her father writes like her mother

Mummy in Haiku too

after we lost mum
her beloved garden beds
returned to seedling

Chapter VI

Zipporah

Until you make the unconscious conscious,
it will direct your life, and you will call it fate.

Carl Jung

Author's note: the following chapter is dedicated to
all who are brave enough to heal and wise enough to let go

Free Association

trigger warning

these
\words/

are   loaded

with
cultural
saltpetre

they   contain

tracings
\of/

tribal
orbital
vertical
residual
torsional
horizontal
\egaugnal/

anemology

said the psychic to the tea-leaf reader,
said the tea-leaf reader to the palmist,
said the palmist to the mind-reader
said the mind-reader to the neighbourhood clairvoyant.
said the clairvoyant to my injured ego…
"lust-drunk, sexually hyped overrated polyamorous schlepping poet!"
"Lassie, you need therapy,
deep
steep
leap
sweep
weep
therapy."

A well-rounded Northcote clairvoyant doubling down on her limerick hitherto dispensed unto me the indispensable in exchange of two Unaipon polymer banknotes. By hook or crook, I was led to a therapist, but not just any run of the mill shrink, far from it, I had landed face down and arse up on the chaise longue of a psychoanalyst whose speciality was lock picking the great subterranean continent of the unconscious. Well, what are you waiting for?

Turn the page!

Moving through five long strong winds… I discovered one brave

therapist inside a Melbournian

gale force of uncompromising truth – one word, three syllables

Zip-por-ah

Wife of Moses

Zipporah — Hebrew for "bird" / "little bird" / "free spirit"

Zipporah, daughter of Jethro – prince and priest of Midian

Zipporah, mother of Gershom, Eliezer

Zipporah, wife of Moses

\/

Zipporah

psychoanalyst / therapist / tissue holder / mirror holder

and sometime thorn in the flesh to Yvette

"I eat women like you for brunch,
and as fortune would have it
in the city of Melbourne,
I am otherwise known as a late riser" — yhh

Transference, Projection, Resistance

Where to commence?

But the beginning is such a mess.

There are no flowers in the attic
only decaying seasons.

I imagine turning ninety-nine years of age
would be easier than turning forty?

Zipporah is rather worldly,
intimidatingly beautiful in
her size six David Jones,
Bourke Street off-the-rack
winter-sale attire.
Yes, indeed
I have known
women like
Zipporah most
of my adult life,
or so I thought?

The mind rambles.
The mouth bites back like a 1980s
soft-porn silent film screening without captions
rattling the undercarriage of my once all and mighty
yet now malleable hopscotch kinetic tongue.

Ho-hum, "**analysis**" is so not for the faint of heart.

One memorable day I overheard an "elephant"
announcing to his mates that he had put
$50 aside just in case he needed to
rent a prostitute for the night on
his inaugural lads weekend visit
to the Gold Coast (1984).

I ask my mother, *mum what is a
prostitute – and how can I rent
one?*

Roast beef & baked spuds
hit the kitchen floor with
little sign of resurrection
mother snaps
*You are never to watch Hill Street Blues ever again.
Missy, do you hear me!*

Unlike mother, I only watched
HSB for the opening theme, it
was catchy as fark.

Father enters the kitchen
dad is really very hungry,
I can see it in his old-world
greenish blueish eyes
as he plates up the gravy,
thyme brushed onions
peas, carrots
Jap pumpkin
& surrendering
Brussels sprouts,

cursing the seriously succulent
razzmatazz roast beef
under his breath,
father gives thanks for his wife,
God, his children,
the perfect golfing weather,
the roof over our head
and the cooked carcass
lying dormant on the disinfected
kitchen linoleum floor,
that no child wants to eat.

I confess to Zipp,
timing is everything.
I could never stomach
Sunday roasts.

Dead animals on
the dinner plate
grew me digestively
intolerant to nursery
rhyme characters.

Zipporah's pen refuses
to recline.

The only overnight *rental*
I had ever heard of was
either Beta or VHS at the
local video store.
And in our suburban 4077
village
VHS won tapes down.

I tell Zipp that following
the traditional family
Sunday roast meat
dropping debacle,
I was banned from watching any
crime-time television shows for
the entire remainder of that year.
Period!

It was the easiest time I ever
served, considering we were
midway through the month of
November.

That was until *Cagney & Lacey*
hit the mid-80s television screens.
And then I went all female gaga
with an out of this world obsession
over Detective Christine Cagney
of the 14th Precinct.
The compulsive obsessive and
long-range metabolising guilt
which I carried for Cagney/Gless
lasted some four seasons or so.

I confess to Zipp that throughout my most
turbulent teen years, mother prayed
constantly for me and father improved
his handicap to a solid ten chipping toward
an eight for one whole entire season.

FYI, I don't think that the land mammal
in paragraphs passing had neither
the stones nor tusk to do anything
of the sort with or without a
sex worker in 1984 – after all,
Jumbo was more or less irrelephant.

Fifty minutes is up!
I survived my very first
psychoanalytical session.

Time sure does fly when
you haven't yet
really begun.

Zipp and I shake hands ":" a dead fish palm exchange…

See you next week!

Shadow Work

Shadow of the Night

I have walked barefoot

in the slowest of motions

through the most desolate

darkest

decrepit

depraved

shadows of the living night.

Be certain not to tilt me.

I shadow

The concept of self individuation
sears me with erosion, withdrawal,
avoidance,
contradiction.

I observe life repressing all around
on a merry-go-round
with carousel horses
too dead to giddy-up.

Doctor They/Them Who
prescribes me
over-the-counter
enteric coated lollies.

The good Doctor orders me to take one,
three times daily,
come back in two months.

I decide to paper-plane the print-out prescription
inbound towards Archerfield Airport on sunset,
preferring instead to
self-medicate on poetry
and a discreet warm body.

In the Middle of Analysis

In the middle of the night
in the middle of a shared pandemic
I lay on my back not falling to pieces

in the middle of the clay-pans
in the middle of three-ways
I am falling into peace

concealing my eyes in the middle of rapture
inhaling their Requiem of silence in D Minor
I frolic in the middle of denial

if it pleases the jury of midnight recovery
and all that glitters is not quite sold
I crave the cravings of my Jewish lover
her middle-finger figure-skating around
the outskirt of my arching sovereign mouth

over there, where – against the rocks of
somebody else's songlines
she and her gather well-heeled
in the middle of an open fire-engine-red
chaise longue

pressing if we must
into scalloped watercolours
dividing rehearsals all over again,
and again, and again

in the middle of a raftless desert-sea
I catch a fallen star from the ankle of
a petulant Milky Way
placing it firmly inside
my lover's middle pocket

in the middle of nowhere
yet someone else's somewhere
remunerating each other's
unravelling limbs in dialogue
for spare body parts
suddenly, in the middle of the most
unordinary stanza
I choose to release her Hebrew stare

in the middle of a shared odyssey
halfway through mid-sentence
syphoning the foam
between Scylla and Charybdis

ego aside
my therapist survives

whilst I, the sometime poet
by the bye return to my lovers'
unpublished womb

Chaise Longue

If you could be any tree
what would you be?

A needle-bearing
cone-producing
pyramidal shaped
sunlight pining
native foliage cypress.

Too soon?

No.
Not at all.
That's your truth.
Let's work with that.

What's the first thing that comes to
mind when you hear the word
addiction?

Sex.
Lots and lots.
Like a Sunny Boy Ekka show bag
I'll show you mine if you show me yours.

Allow me to cut straight
to the organic tofu.

I don't vape.
I don't drink.
I don't smoke.
I don't gamble.

I don't do drugs.
I seldom flatulate.

And I gave up
autobiographical
stalking last century.

So, yep.

You want transparency Zipp,
well, I'm being completely
confidentially
intimately
painfully
brutally
honest.

Sex.

indoors, outdoors.

art galleries.

rooftops.

basements.

half a night at the mausoleum.

beaches so passé de mode.

Sex for me has been

both an eclectic verse and a horsedrawn hearse.

Zipporah, her annoyingly spotless porcelain French Suisse Polish face,

now bone-dry expressionless.

Mouth wincingly agape.

!!!!!!!!!!!!!!!!!!!!!!

Jaw descending beneath the Fitzroyian Persian covered floor rug.

!!!!!!!!!!!!!!!!!!!!!!

mental sticky-note #1:
Never interrupt deadpan deafening silence

!!!!!!!!!!!!!!!!!!!!!

mental sticky-note #2:
Zipp's biro, nailed to its midriff.

!!!!!!!!!!!!!!!!!!!!!

mental sticky-note #3
Not even inside the capsule of one's own pathology
could I escape the hedging of my own subconscious.

"----------------------"

Fifty-five minutes up!

Time sure does fly
when you haven't
yet really begun.

Zipp and I shake hands ":" a limp fish palm exchange…

See you next week!

a view of one's own

eaves bloat with a thousand
suburban autumns

rain gathers
abstract capacity

blue frog
begs for a new coat
at the pinch of summer

moss rivals thirsty water tank

a verandah door for the most
part
forgets how to open its eyes

not all the time,
just for the rest of time.

awnings overhang
with inverse
enjambments;

the family home bites
its upper immutable lip
with unreserved
poetic
clout;

sinking further into stumps
of creative, depressive isolation

gurgling an atlas for breakfast

lorikeets vow never to return.

Egyptian thread count

Forty-four minutes before you boarded
the plane from Melbourne to Cairo,
I forgot to tell you that I was already
waiting for you in the cradle of
civilisation.

While you were fumbling with
Melbournian 'farewells'
I swam beneath the desert skin
some twelve thousand
four hundred kilometres
over two nights, with your
sixth-generation iPod touch
tucked soundly, neatly
within the holiest fold
of my left breast.

Swallowing seas whole and
chowdering on whalebone
villanesque soup nineteen lines over
all along an otherworldly ocean way,
spirit torpedoed me
towards you,
to be with you,
to protect you,
to hear your throbbing crimson
heart beating only for me
in the land of a thousand
secret valleys.

Before you arrived, I had already seen
your face everywhere in Egypt –
coffee stables, nearby the Gulf, long
walks, spilt wine, short cries, galleries

your passport photo lit up a thousand
and one billboards, I revelled inside
each one
of them;

the beginning of the end is so cliché

At least, I think it was you.

untitled 2017

#1

i learn how to be you

and you relearn me.

#2

free free free

as birds circling

over fawkner cemetery.

#3

driving through

metallic skies,

i will get along without you.

T:4:2

Poetry is something in-between the dream and its interpretation – Lou Andreas-Salomé

Last night in Fitzroy
I hosted my very first
tea party
the gathering itself was
Edwardian with a
Gertrude splash
of Victorian,

a simple caffeine-free
non-virtue signaling
backyard leaf
nothing less
something more
bookish
nervish
nerdish
tea party.

Over one century ago
I wrote, lick-sealed
and posted exactly five
invitations sent via par avion
from the original former
Fitzroy Post Office
St Georges Road.

No ifs.
No butts.
No Alexander Bell phone-a-friend.

I had not yet manifested
Zipporah into the elevating
future of mind and critical time.

In anticipation of this
cardamom themed
brewing shindig,
obsessively I over prepared
where the lavenders grow wild
former Fitzroyian
post-renovated
pre-pandemic
two bedrooms
workers cottage
to stellar beauty.

The chimneystack was stacked to the heavens
with cloves, cinnamon, vanilla, ginger cuttings
and one lone occasional side table keeping company with an empty
art nouveau faux crystal glass vase in maiden desire of a good
Phar Lap stem.

The dining table was prepared with an assortment
of crumbled hand-rolled chickpeas mint balls
and lentil patties hors d`oeuvres,

tea-lit candles lined the entrance hall
akin to a bookcase tarmac
the was sun was descending
the evening was set.

Alas, Rilke did not RSVP.

Bachelard was buried
beard-deep within his own
commanding framework
of poetical elements –
water
fire
air
earth.

Freud was a late scratching
and Nietzsche promised
to drop by with a wrist full
of native pig-face edibles to fill
my vacant vase
at around 11pm
but only if he could.

And yes, you guessed it,
Friedrich could not.

In total attendance for the
tea-leaf party
that only left myself and none
other than...
{insert drumroll here please}

Lou Andreas-Salomé.

Lou who had RSVP'd me some ninety
years in advance; and now, here she
was standing at the front door in
breathtaking
je ne sais quoi beauty and attendance.

Moving through the yardage of
scones and yuzu pear conserve,
dear Lou, quite literally began spilling
the tea on a life well anointed in her field
as the first female psychoanalyst –
novelist, essayist, poet, continental muse,
social feminist agitator,

philosopher of religion,
gendered psychiatry,
female independence and her
expert pioneering defense for
sexual
liberation.

Lou, just sitting right there,
in front of me, nonchalantly
leafing through her very own
extraordinary herstory with
unfencing tenacious certitude
oh-so cavalierly, so deliberately,
so – so – so
erotically matter of factly.

I, a self-confessed intellectual
lightweight
clung onto her every consonant
for dear life,
stoned cold and tea sober I began
stumbling over her every vowel.

Here I am and there I was, tossing
back each and every delicate tea-sip
into the district throat of no return;
all the while entangling myself more
and more into Lou's seemingly
endless quotative universe.

The night grew long,
my hair grew longer,
the teas were flowing.

For a singular fleeting moment
I had noticed that the
double bone China serving platter
sprinkled generously with smoked
paprika began gyrating beneath my
curved Lebanese cucumber cutlet,
add to this a chorus line of
lime spinach & capsicum chutney
inspired cupcakes
donated with influential culinary
inquiry from the
As You Like it
Merry Wives of Windsor
All's Well That Ends Well
inseparable thespian couple
two-doors-down
were now appearing rather zestful,
convivial and dare I suggest
imperiously entertaining.

Darkness soon branched upon
Fitzroy,
my tea party unanimously drew to
an exquisite serviette end.

I walked Lou to her awaiting chariot
aka psychoanalytical time-husk
on the corner of Brunswick Street North,
I thanked her for attending my
tea party
knowing how very busy she is back home;
what with dodging misogynistic tea bullets
left, centre and right

and guarding her interplanetary
heavyweight intellectualism
evening and night / light and day.

Momentarily, I thought, until we meet
again friend: but who was I kidding?
Again – was an oxymoronic position by default,
this was after all
my past
my dream
my future
my dilemma
my returning
I was the sole captainess of my
loose-leaf destiny.

An anonymous premonition
that not even I could have predicted
way back when.

~~To Let~~

i exist inside worlds

that only few

are ever permitted to visit

""

eviction is not an option

girl, intercepted

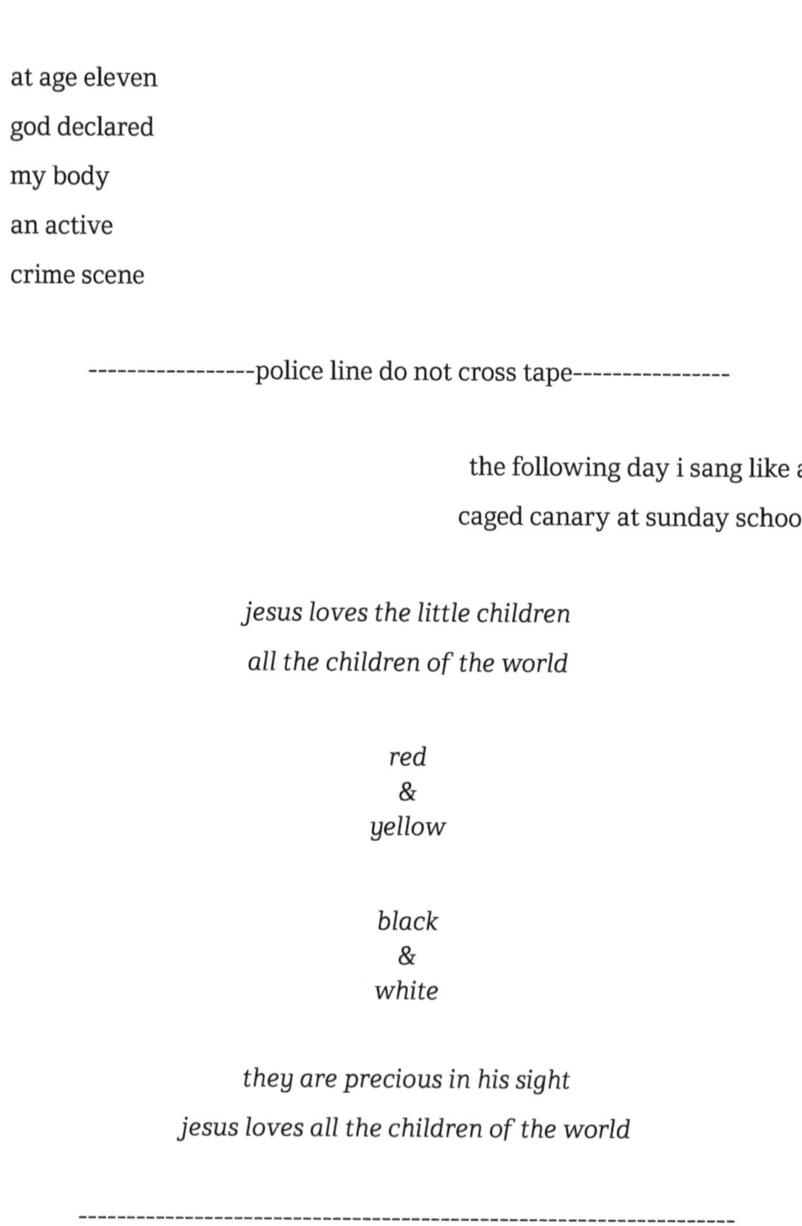

at age eleven
god declared
my body
an active
crime scene

----------------police line do not cross tape----------------

the following day i sang like a
caged canary at sunday school

jesus loves the little children
all the children of the world

red
&
yellow

black
&
white

they are precious in his sight
jesus loves all the children of the world

LOVE

love
love
love
love
love
love
love
love
love
love
love
love
love
love
love
love
love
love
love

I will. I can. I do. I am.

Chapter VII

Note Bene

I am not what happened to me, I am what I choose to become

Carl Jung

Lettera 32 (1964)

Sylvia Plath once typed out the chasm of her mind on a Lettera 32, as too do I

You ask me to type out
just how deeply I feel about you,
about us,
I tell you sincerely there is simply
not enough ink to absorb within
the capillaries of this unspooling
ribbon on how exactly I feel about us,
about you.

I am full of contradictions, unmetered
galaxies, semicolons that go bump in
the night & unyielding ellipses that
know far, far too much.

And now – oh how, this limited edition
powder-blue steel Olivetti Lettera 32,
presenting in immaculate
mechanical qwertyuiop

thwack
clack
clickety
clack

has spoken from beyond the
inamorata headstone of
translucent onion skin paper
in aureate volume
time and time again

The Belle ~~Jar~~

deeply surrendering

notes upon air

ghost river gum

trephina gorge

arrival next morn

breathlessly

exposed

beneath apricot stars

subconscious soliloquy

unfurling

dew collarbones

two halves

one whole

surrendering deeply

Ars Poetica

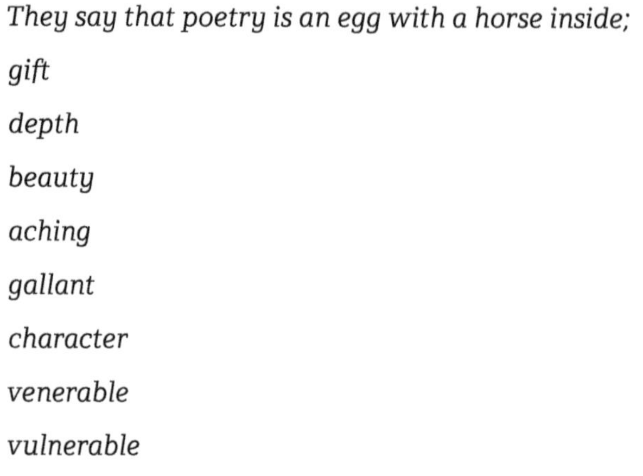

They say that poetry is an egg with a horse inside;
gift
depth
beauty
aching
gallant
character
venerable
vulnerable

I say, crack me a Bucephalus omelette please ————
and then binocular me while I bareback albumen spirit
decantering flesh of poetry from within these swollen
chambers of an unframed trotting mind.

To the Nth Degree

Never ever have I
sprained tongue
so intentionally
so justifiably
so insatiably
then with you

not with any /ˈwʊmən/ or /mæn/

do not pass go
do not hit pause
just let repeat
if only for a circular millennium

m
y

l o v e

If in Doubt

When you run out of brassieres to unclasp
Levi's to unbutton
corners to turn
and people to blame

"

When there is not enough carry-on
room for duty-free Botanical Gin
38,000 feet above "see" level

"

When every poem you write feels as though it
is eviscerating you through the
Sydney literati mud

"

when it feels as though you are all but
surrendering to the mesh of
unpublished shadows whom
have penned less before you

"

Remember.

You can always hide inside the bosom
of my jangling writer's closet, you know where the key is¿

cover of mine

i gaze upon ocean
the way you

insect my legs

hunger
fever
damp
necessary

for every touch
there is a season

for every hush
there is a reason

stretch like chalazae
lover of mine,

take me there
beyond the cover

decalcify me

Lit Clique

Beware the thought police
are at large – said one
author to the other,
where, I care said the publisher
to the poet – at the bar,
in the tearoom, bathroom,
behind the desk, behind the
microphone, watering the plastic
palm trees in the foyer, where?
They're in plain clothes,
they are everywhere whispered
the bookseller to the illustrator.

Cornered at the vegetarian
countertop,
I am asked curiously, politely,
yet not so surprisingly –
Yvette Henry Holt, what say
your pronouns…?
Confessing my grammatical
sins in the green room while
tooth wrestling parsley on a
vegan artisan multigrain sanger
at a high-altitude writers' festival

was never a thing until it became

a thing.

Nonetheless, I have been asked a

rather direct question, thereby I will

attempt to answer
with a rather direct response.

[mental cap locks are on]

I announce my pronouns

me
myself
and *I*

swallowing the sabbath air without

soda water, you could have heard a

pulp free recycled napkin fall,

I continue...

My pronouns are all lowercase
except for the I as it is a
stand-alone pronoun,
some say this is what makes the
letter majuscule 'I' so unique to the
English language.

Go finger I conclude...but what I
really meant to say was *go figure!*

[insert double chin stroke here]

Atop the Azure Mountains,
some miniscule moments following
I thought I heard a misgendered volcanic
bobb~~y ie~~-pin sigh,
but then again, I must have mis-herd.
Suddenly the green room blushed
a whiter shade of spring.

The October 2023 writers' festival,
sure, it was wild but not that wild...
It wasn't like Oscar Wilde or anything,
more like Jiminy Cricket wild
"Always let your conscience be your guide." JC

hands
f
r
e
e

"
more fool you

for trusting only

my hands

it is through poetry

"
that i truly braille

`I; "don't,,,:know

I will marry you someday
I told you so, as you blew
out all thirty candles
on your thirty-fourth birthday.

Someday we just might exchange
biblical vows before cardinal eyes
of papal cloth,
be certain to wear your
great-great-great-grandmother's
Irish linen foam-stained Boston
bound pearl ivory button dress.

I just might marry you someday,
    – tie the knot(s) in my stomach
    – in sickness and in health
    – for richer for poorer
    – forsaking all others
    – for always

We just might move with sun, moon
and tin whistle across the re-echoing
malty bruising Muir Éireann
and in addition
we just might
arrive at Anglesey and rise south
with attentive black guillemots as
they merrily gait
about their nosey business
by cliffs and prey.

Yes, Anglesey
where I shall wrap you in poetry
and paper-towel you with
infringed beauty
proclaiming *I Do*
to the local publican, baker,
butcher, fishmonger,
bookseller and
candlestick maker.

Anglesey, where we just might
tower and fall at the
barefoot soles of unmade
seagrass beds and
neogothic leatherback turtles
milli metering our way
across brooming dunes of
shingle
sands
all the while jig sawing each
other's
lower torsos at a glacier pace
bound only by saltmarsh
witnessed by drapes
for an entire generational
hamlet eternity.

And yes, perhaps, just maybe,
we will honeymoon at

Holyhead

and through grit milk molars
I shall clench thresher, dace
and whelk
for dinner every evening
without emotional stammer.

I promise to debone and dethrone
all signs of
life
until fresh caught flesh is all
but a mere
descendant
of memory.

Our fireplace will gasp carbon
neutrality, terry tea-towels will
be ironed and folded
into secular handkerchief squares,
assuredly with grand confidence
the peppermill will
be sabotaged with an indecent
amount of sub-continent clove.
My lovely, you are without a sliver
of gunpowder Irish gin doubt
the absolute Kerry Pippin
of my visionary third eye.

I think that I will marry you
someday,
but then again,
my most alluring
emerald isle gemstone,
you know what they say
about some…day.

Someday, it will all make sense.

Untitled

I never want to *fall* in love again.

Rather, I want to rise in love.

To fall is to descend.

To *rise* is infinite.

K-k-k-*indle*

I have a confession to make
some ladies are like books
hardcover
softback
trade cloth
textbook
e-pub
chap book
leather bound
paperback
classic fold
bargain basement
beautifully bound
well-worn to the spine
some even arrive in a renewable removable dust jacket – optional!
Who knew?

Vintage dog-eared to the clutching pearl lobes,
creased only ever so slightly toward the corners of
page-turning crow's feet with powdery lemony
acknowledgements and some are more or less an
incorrigible page turner.

But not this one – Oh no, not at all.

This one was more or less an e-reader of the highest
ninety per cent recycled magnesium order.
This one shone bright in darkness and in light.

Truth be told this one had me at the seven-day free trial
cancel anytime subscription,
i.e. pay now or forever hold your
credit card details peace here.

This one was not your average everyday library garden
variety type either, this one was reddit popular nonplussed
with select upgrade premium features at the ready, always
responsive to my lingering full-length screwdriver
fingerprint touch without freezing or bugging.

This one, all of 6.7 inches from comforting forehead
to deluxe bezzle chin with its *never let me go* Wi Fi grip
held a whole lot more under that slick slate grey hood
than the online 'just bought' Amazonian reviewers ever
reviewed.

This e-reader could go on and on and on and on for weeks
without fear nor famish of recharging her signature stealth
minimally layered surface
albeit via an outdated micro-USB cable.

Uncomplaining of place, adjusting to whatever
time-zone I moved with,
by the pool she splashed,
a frolicking flirt at the Business Class Lounge
she flashed.

K-k-k-*indle…*
The mere mention of her magnanimous name had me
swiping from chapter to chapter without lag from
sunrise to sun-get.

Slightly higher priced than that of her leading
competitors thought I
but toe-to-tap,
she was well worth the ad hoc monthly deduction.

A head-turner from back to font with superior engineering
attention to detail,
easy on the eye
and unable to fry
this one's towering geek bones
and anti-glare smudge-free tinting cover
preserved her curves well from imposing foreign rays.

Left to right
north to south
with a magnetic whisper of a mouth
this one held firm and loyal to my everyday
wish list favourites.
Ergonomically sleek,
this one was an all-round digital delight to pillow
cradle in between my midlife crisis of dark mode and
content organisation versus annotation.

Able to go anywhere
anytime
any space
K-k-kindle was a definite thumbs-up one of a membership kind.

Black on the edges and paperwhite on the inside,
just the way I hike it.

Poetry, fiction, fantasy, biographical, thriller, self-help
autobiographical, sci-fi, literary non-fiction, horror,
chick-lit, magical realism, speculative fiction, crime,
memoir, and history to name but a few genres were at
the top of her 'still looking' just one click away to unlock unlimited
bestsellers and much, much more.

For a fugacious moment in time, this one brought balance, convenience,
reliability, and functionality with an inbuilt gloating internal memory of
one whole 32 gigabytes – that was, until she could debit me no more.

It is oh-so true, this stylish one had predicted my search engine long
before in perpetuity I could purchase hers.

Aaaah, yes, say it with me, altogether now **K-k-k-*indle***
was far more demanding than I had ever really bought her credit for.

Moral of the spiel, never judge a book...by its removable cover!

19straighty8

A psychoanalytical meltdown for the wake-me-up before-you go-go ages.

Hey, hey it was a Saturday night (1988)

Flack vs Coverdale throwback.

Last word, Van Morrison.

Generation X uncut

3

2

1

~~

Mute MTV
more *Killing Me Softly*
less *Here I Go Again.*

~~

More *strumming my brain with his fingers*
less Riccadonna
more *all flushed with fever.*

~~

Big hair
medium smile
long tee shirts
short Daisy Dukes
knee-high leg warmers.
Just the way you liked it
when my brothers weren't home.

~~

I heard he sang a good song,
I heard he had a style.

~~

Do not sook.
Do not sweat.
Do not colonise my tailbone.

~~

And there he was this young boy
a stranger to my eyes

~~

Do not coffee me at 3am.
Do not touch the CD player.
Do not bite the hand that needs you.

~~

Hold me.
Leave.
Stay.

~~

Cameo appearance

Enter

Orchestral Manoeuvres in the Dark OMD

If you leave, I won't cry, I won't shed one single tear

~~

Whitesnake
to his *Brown Eyed Girl*
Is This Love?
Because I'm going down the only road I've ever known.

~~

Once upon a shrine,

wooden fences made bi-curious neighbours.

~~

Strumming his pain with my fingers.

Writing my life with his song.

~~

Postscriptum.

~~

January 2025

I saw you just the other day,
my, how you have grown.

~~

. .
,

Between the Lines,

Friend, just confirming —

You are not really reading these pages; you know that right?

This book, these pages, – are literally reading you.

To be continued…

Chapter VIII

Typewriting

Loveth even your frenemies

yhh

Never Again

Following October 7,
I wept like a baby too
heavy in tears to be
changed.

never again

I cried in Hebrew for
weeks.

never again

What does that even
sound like?

never again

What does that even
taste like?

never again

What does that even
mean?

never again

It means that we will
never ever forget.

It means that all
hostages must be
released and returned
to their families.

never again

It means that we shall sing
again.

It means that we will dance
again.

It means that someday,
I will *write* again.

Never Again Is Now!

Not tomorrow, now!

And you, dare I ask, what
will you do *never again*?

bread **Sticks &** ancient **Stones**

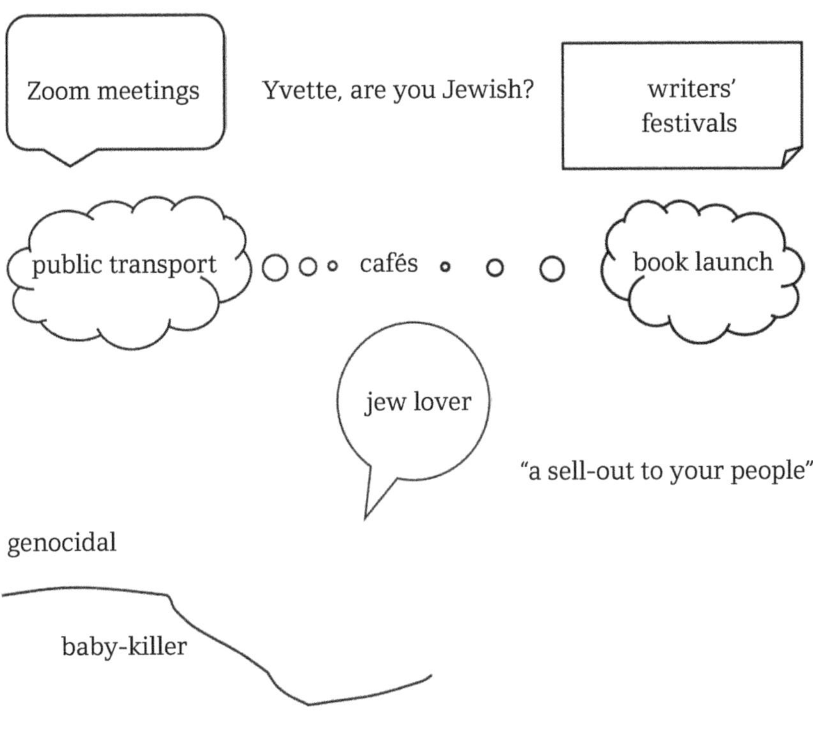

Calling all Zionists
Cancel all Zionists
Cancel all multi-multi
award-winning Jewish
musicians who have
given their blood, sweat
and tears to the Australian
music industry (DC)

In fact, just cancel all artistic
Jews

Cancel all Indigenous writers,
performers, creative artists
who dare speak, hug, coffee
or so much as smile at Jews

Cancel anyone who did not walk across the bridge,
repeat, cancel anyone who did not walk across the bridge
(*Roger That. 10-4 Big Daddy*)

Cancel anyone who even dares to dream of waving an Australian flag,
especially in their sleep, beware of the Dream Police,
(come now Yvette) that was such a Cheap Trick (*Negatory*)

On second thought, just cancel
all cancels this click bait pile on
is getting confusing!?
(*Copy That*)

your family must be so ashamed of you…

black c***

you are the first aboriginal jew lover I have ever met, I didn't know people like you even existed…

as a proud aboriginal indigenous native black sovereign woman of colour
who loveth even her frenemies
I say to you…
same shite, different century
bread sticks and ancient stones

Sabbatical 2025

My mid-life creative gap-year

A daughter, mother, grandmother.
protective, loving, cooking, reading, basketball, playgrounds, long walks,
fitness, time togetherness

A true and loyal friend.
travel, coffees, bookstores, long phone calls, guidance, volunteering,
thermal hot springs, short walks

A walk with multifaith.
daily prayers, scriptures, awareness, forgiveness, reading, faith, handwriting,
typewriting, very long walks

In *spirit*

I am global. I am tribal.

I am. *Love*

Ruptured (the contents of) mash-up

Thirty-six eminent contributors. Thirty-six compelling essays as titled.

I am a Jew
We Are Still Here
Against Silence
Writing in the Time of War
Warrior of Words
Nana's Bracelet
A Stone Under History's Wheel
A Rant and a Recipe
My Kitchen Sanctuary
The Winner
Boiled Eggs
Pickle Project

The Women's Circle
A Daily Update
A Message from My Friend
I'm Not Antisemtic, But...
The End of Ignorance
The Crack and the Light
Pacing the Stage
The Woman in the Arena
Police Report
The Privilege of Being a Pacifist
In Case I Ever Get Kidnapped
Who Will Hide my Daughter?
Open Hiding

Walls
(Un)safe
North of the River
Hanging on by a Thread
Jewish Enough
What Hurts More?
The Pain of Others
Nothing Antisemtic Here
October 7 Diary
And Still We Dance
Faith Over Fear

Chapter IX

Cultural Phenomenology

The *Blackfella*

I am, I said it, I know it, I own it

I am the *blackfella* who was born into an expansive family of exceptional black love.

I am that *blackfella* who grew up the youngest of five children, raised at the kitchen dining table of superior black knowledge encompassing storytelling literature, sporting excellence, higher education, politics, justice, ancestral discourses of rivers, lands, skies and spiritual environments.

I am the *blackfella* who was raised listening to her parents, aunts and uncles at the altar of deep respect, manners, attention to detail and humility.

We, like so many families in our tight-knit, pruned carnations, manicured lawns' south-western suburban community are that *blackfella* family who grew up in multiple worlds of neighbourhood camaraderie uprising in the pursuit of equitable educational and social community development for students and elders; I am that *blackfella* who benefited from parental hard yakka and home ownership borne from working-class grit built into the sandstones of intergenerational fingernails. For such families it was never just another day in the colony, Inala East 4077 *was* the colony, the colony of neighbouring champions who rolled sleeves up and gave it an almighty fair go. My parents and neighbouring families were not flash nor flushed with bungoo, to the contrary, they scrimped and scraped their way through those earlier years to provide for their children what they never had.

Today, Inala is a thriving multi-lingual melting-pot of who's who *blackfellas*, whitefellas and faces from lands I had only ever read about from cover to cover every other weekend at the local council library corner (of Rosemary and Abelia streets) throughout the Hawkeism, Thatcherism, Reaganism '80s. That was the Inala I grew up in.

4077 continues to grow as a large sprawling inter-generational, internationally celebrated multicultural suburb with enormous vibrant public festivals held throughout the year highlighting Australian history and diverse cultural community gatherings while maintaining with gusto its proud strengthening indigenous roots.

Am I not doubly blessed to have been born and raised by two immeasurable parents whose bloodlines are now my grandchildren's collective story lines. Am I not doubly blessed that our shared herstory\history without deviation or pause pulsates beneath the consciousness of a salient cultural growth from one generation to the next.

Moving in silence throughout south-east, western, central and far north Queensland; my parents' ancestral lands speak directly to me through night skies, totemic marsupials and otherworldly birds whose feathers and skins continue to roam the wishbones of these lands – just as they did once upon a dusk.

Quietly footsteps walk beside me, they protect me, they guide me, shhh – in *clevering* way, *blackfella* old ways, *spirit* walk with me.

The *Clevering*

Yvette Henry Holt
granddaughter of
a stockman, a lore man
a clever woman, a bush-medicine woman.

I am that *blackfella* who heralds from
four phenomenal Aboriginal grandparents.

I do not speak on behalf of other *blackfellas*
and nor do I presume to.

I speak with the tongue of my mother and the rod of my father.

I life on inherent
phenomenological
cultural ways of being...

I walk with a *blackfella*ness
in ways that move
without dialogue
watch me
watch you – watch me.

The *clevering* and when you know.

You know.

Chapter X

Home

I am deliberate and afraid of nothing.

Audre Lorde

ˋhōm

home*coming*

home*land*

home*stead*

home*owner*

home*made*

home*front*

home*work*

home*maker*

home*town*

home*grown*

home*ly*

home*spun*

home*sick*

home*page*

home*body*

home*run*

home is where the *heart* splinters

home is where the *heal*ing begins

For Dad, our journey together continues, your hand inside mine, we got this Pop – forever.

Chapter XI

Final Word

So, can you keep a secret?

Well, can you?

Notes

'Suburban Lighthouse': Heathcliff, Emily Brontë, *Wuthering Heights*, 1847; Edgar Allan Poe, 'A Dream Within a Dream', 1849

'The Tower of Blue Horses' refers to the painting of that name by Franz Marc, 1913

'Ross River': Wakaman – maternal grandmother, 1917–1949

'4077 The Derive': 'Theory of the Dérive' by Guy Debord, 1956; 'This is the mother-love, which is one of the most moving and unforgettable memories of our lives', C.G. Jung

'Memphis, Tennessee': The line 'rear vision never lies' is from Yvette Holt, 'The River City', *Anonymous Premonition*, University of Queensland Press, 2008

'Heptonstall, West Yorkshire': the text quoted at the end is on the headstone of Sylvia Plath Hughes

'4078': 'the WWII US Army ordnance depot' – see Mapping Brisbane History website, https://mappingbrisbanehistory.com.au/

'19straighty8': 'Killing Me Softly', Roberta Flack, 1973; 'Here I Go Again', Whitesnake, *1987*; 'If You Leave', OMD Orchestral Manoeuvres in the Dark, *1986*; 'Brown Eyed Girl', Van Morrison, 1967; 'Is This Love?', Whitesnake, *1987*

'girl, intercepted': 'Jesus Loves the Little Children' by C. Herbert Woolston

'Ars Poetica': Horace, 'The Art of Poetry', c.19 BC

Ruptured, Jewish Women in Australia Reflect On Life Post-October 7 – Kofman Dr Lee, Paluch Tamar
Published by Lamm Jewish Library of Australia (LJLA) 2025

'The *Blackfella*': 'bungoo' meaning money in Aboriginal English

Acknowledgements

All that you read between these covers did not come about by creative alchemy and lentil bread alone; to the contrary all that I have consciously scaffolded arrived via intense and at times painful, painful therapy; self-reflection, denial, ugliness of circumstances and ripened beauty of ageless truth disco-mirrored into a mocktail of meteoric metaphors. Like many of you, I too have loved passionately and lost monumentally. If you take anything out of this collection, then take this – I never ran with wolves nor she-wolves, not once. Instead, my one quick fix poison was to marathon with my very own shadows of the dastardly living night: for decades I was spilling in countries, cities and deserts that rocked my insatiable leaky boat without a life jacket in sight. Now, as I inchingly release the compression of memory, I acknowledge that some fifteen years of writing have been caged into the contents of *Fitzroy North 3068*. But wait, there is more.

I offer you bits and pieces of my life story, a casement view of watch pocket psychogenic compassing not as a conical measurement to therapy nor as a sip-tip to fair medicine – but as an invitation to witness through my language, the soul to these eyes; a fleeting moment to taste life twice – with me.

What *Fitzroy North 3068* revealed to me throughout the longest of seasons is that I am neither a patient nor client to anything or anyone.

I am a sometime visitor to thyself.

With *spirit*, I simply am!

I would like to thank family, friends and colleagues for their encouragement, enthusiasm, support and love throughout the internal harvesting of this collection; to those who stood by me through thick and skin of the pre-publishing process for the book you are now holding, I say, thank you. To my immediate family – my beautiful grandchildren, the absolute supernovas of my universe who let me off the hook more times than they care to remember with our regular weekend hikes, prized library days, basketball challenges, home-cooking depot in the family kitchen, creative and prayerful conversations while I shawled distractively deep into my writing almost every other weekend over the last eighteen months without reprieve. To Kevin-Bailey, Harper, Arnica, you now have me all to yourselves until the next manuscript is well overdue, with all my love, Gan'gang. To my daughter

Cheyenne, thank you for all the early morning coffee and avocado toast drop-offs throughout the assemblance of this manuscript and for sharing your most poignant memories and conversations about your Nan – all my love, mum. To my courageous handsome, stately elderly father – Albert Holt III to whom I owe so much of the woman I have become because of the man he became; Dad, I love you (we got this Pop).

FNAWN First Nations Australia Writers Network I pay tribute to all our First Nation fellow writers who continuously lead the way with their exemplary writing and very necessary publications of Aboriginal and Torres Strait Islander literature, illustrators, storytellers and of course poets. To Samantha Faulkner, a sincere thank you for your longstanding support and friendship.

To my Jewish sisters and brothers, for all your ongoing support and care of each other, of us – Lee Kofman; thank you for all that you do to promote Australian Jewish women's voices, stories and publication so bravely, so tirelessly, in solidarity of our unwavering sisterhood, your tears are my tears. Matrilineal. Ruptured. Healing.

A special note to so say a big thank you of warmth, friendship, loyalty and literary collegiality to Luke Stegemann, Lee Kofman, Michele Seminara, Anna Jacobson, Robbie Coburn and Magan Magan for their fearless testimonials of this collection. You each greatly matter to me.

To the incredible staff and board at the Queensland Writer's Centre, thank you for all your support and bottomless coffee rounds. The QWC – literary trailblazers at large. To my agent Jeanne Ryckmans at Key People Creative Management, with gratitude for all that you do. Thank you to Terri-ann White at Upswell Publishing for standing by this manuscript in all its unrushed disrobing and reshaping, at long last, this collection has found its rightful publishing home. Thank you to Kelly Lee for her astute proofreading and editorial guidance, to Keith Feltham thank you for your typesetting patience throughout this collection – every full stop, every out of sorts em dash, every excessive word spacing, every single keyboard symbol is exactly where it ought to be. To Becky Chilcott from Chil3, thank you for the amazingly seductive magenta splashed cover design of my deliberate three-legged blushing chaise longue.

Special thanks to Jackie Huggins and Marcia Langton for all your unwavering support, and invaluable guidance and love over the years.

To my ethereal Wife of Moses, Zipporah – may you continue to walk with me, almost every step of the way...

This book is dedicated to the memory of my beautiful, beloved, *clever* mother – Marlene.

About Upswell

Upswell Publishing was established in 2021 by Terri-ann White as a not-for-profit press. A perceived gap in the market for distinctive literary works in fiction, poetry and narrative non-fiction was the motivation. In her years as a bookseller, writer and then publisher, Terri-ann has maintained a watch on literary books and the way they insinuate themselves into a cultural space and are then located within our literary and cultural inheritance. She is interested in making books to last: books with the potential to still be noticed, and noted, after decades and thus be ripe to influence new literary histories.

About this typeface

Book designer Becky Chilcott chose Foundry Origin not only as a strong, carefully considered, and dependable typeface, but also to honour her late friend and mentor, type designer Freda Sack, who oversaw the project. Designed by Freda's long-standing colleague, Stuart de Rozario, much like Upswell Publishing, Foundry Origin was created out of the desire to say something new.

www.ingramcontent.com/pod-product-compliance
Ingram Content Group Australia Pty Ltd
76 Discovery Rd, Dandenong South VIC 3175, AU
AUHW021022260226
423902AU00004B/4

9 780645 984071